Lupines Grow In The Cordillera Blanca Mountains

FACES AND PLACES

PERU

BY MARYCATE O'SULLIVAN

THE CHILD'S WORLD®, INC.

GRAPHIC DESIGN AND PRODUCTION
Robert E. Bonaker / Graphic Design & Consulting Co.

PHOTO RESEARCH
James R. Rothaus / James R. Rothaus & Associates

COVER PHOTO
Quechua boy holding a lamb
©Galen Rowell/CORBIS

Library of Congress Cataloging-in-Publication Data
O'Sullivan, MaryCate, 1973–
Peru / by MaryCate O'Sullivan.
p. cm.
Includes index.
Summary: Describes the history, geography, people, and
customs of the South American country, Peru.
ISBN 1-56766-739-2 (lib. bdg. : alk. paper)

1. Peru — Juvenile literature.
[1. Peru.] I. Title.

F2408.5 .O88 2000   99-042409
985 — dc21   CIP

Table of Contents

Earth is a place full of many different things. There are green jungles and dry deserts. There are flat meadows and tall mountains. Some areas are snowy and others are hot. Where on Earth can you find all of these things in one place? Peru!

Peru is a country on the **continent** of South America. It lies along the coast of the Pacific Ocean. The countries of Bolivia, Brazil, Chile, Colombia, and Ecuador are all Peru's neighbors.

Western Hemisphere

Eastern Hemisphere

Both Peru (white) And U.S.A. (green) Are In The West

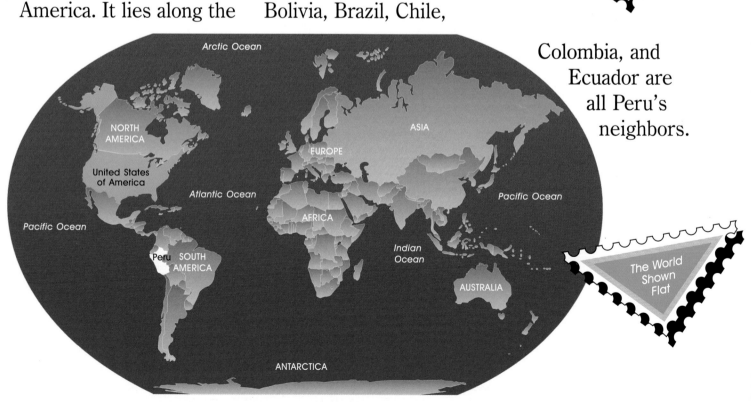

The World Shown Flat

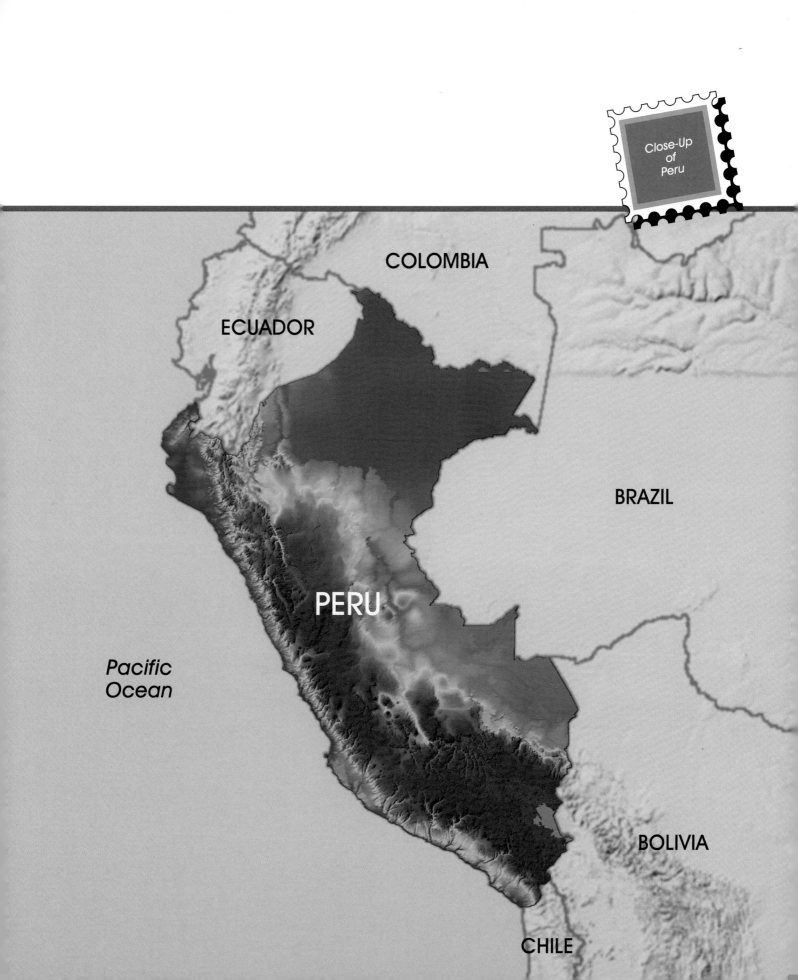

COLOMBIA

ECUADOR

BRAZIL

PERU

Pacific
Ocean

BOLIVIA

CHILE

Close-Up
of
Peru

Waves Crash Onto A Rugged Shoreline South Of Lima

Amazon River

• Pampa Grande

CORDILLERA BLANCA

Lima ★

CORBIS/Tony Arruza

Peru has three types of land: the dry coastal area, the high *Andes Mountains,* and the steamy *Amazon jungle*. The coastal region is mostly dry desert where many of Peru's cities are found.

The steep Andes are farther inland. They rise more than 18,000 feet into the air and have deep canyons between them. Some of the mountains are so tall, they have snow on top of them all year long! The Amazon jungle, or **rain forest,** lies to the east of the Andes. It is an area of thick, green forests and winding rivers.

CORBIS/Kevin Schafer

People Travel By Ferry On The Amazon

Ruins Of A Moche Indian Pyramid Near Pampa Grande

CORBIS/Nathan Benn

Many plants and animals are able to live in Peru's different types of land. Along the coast, sea lions and pelicans hunt and play in the ocean. Hummingbirds and condors are often seen in the higher Andes areas. Llamas and **alpacas** live in the Andes, too. In the Amazon, thousands of types of animals can be found. Bears, monkeys, snakes, jaguars, toucans, and piranhas are just some of the creatures that live in the green forests and rivers of the area.

A Cactus Plant In Bloom In Colca Canyon

Not many types of plants and trees are able to live in the dry or high areas of Peru. But in the hot, sticky weather of the Amazon, thousands of types of plants and trees grow. The jungle grows so thick in places, few people are able to live there.

A Tamandua Anteater On A Tree Branch

Machu Picchu

Colca Canyon

A Brown LLama At The Ruins Of Machu Picchu

Reenacting The Landing Of The First Incas On Lake Titicaca Near Puno

Machu Picchu

Nazca • Puno • Lake Titicaca

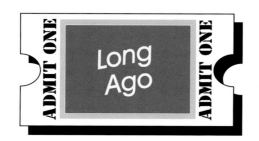
Scientists believe people have been living in Peru for more than 12,000 years. These first people hunted for food and lived in caves for shelter. Over time, many groups learned to farm crops and build houses. Some groups even built cities and societies, or **civilizations**. The earliest civilization in Peru was created by the *Chavín* Indians. Over time, other groups created civilizations, too.

Peru's most important civilization was created by the **Inca** Indians. The Incas built roads and bridges to make traveling easier. They had their own government and their own language— *Quechua* (KECH–wah). They were also great warriors. The Incas defeated many other groups and became very powerful. At one time, the Inca kingdom stretched from Colombia all the way to Chile!

CORBIS/Yann Arthus-Bertrand

This Ancient Drawing On The Land Near Nazca Is So Big, It Can Only Be Seen From The Air

Ruins Of Machu Picchu, An Ancient Inca City In The Mountains

Peru Today

The Incas did not rule for very long. In 1532, a Spanish soldier named Francisco Pizarro sailed to Peru with fewer than 200 men. He was looking for riches he had heard about in stories from other explorers. The Spanish marched deep into the Incas' land, killed their king, and took over the Incas' kingdom. Spain now controlled Peru and its people.

Spain ruled Peru for almost 300 years. Then, in 1820, a man from Argentina named José de San Martín sailed to Peru. He wanted Spain to leave South America. Peruvians joined forces with him and declared their independence from Spain on July 28, 1821. Today, Peru has its own government and its own laws.

President Alberto Fujimori In Lima In 1998

CORBIS/AFP

Francisco Pizarro Landed In Peru In 1532

CORBIS/Bettmann

The Palace Of Justice In Lima

PALACIO DE JVSTICIA

Quechua Girls In Native Dress In Cuzco

Huallanca

★Lima

Cuzco

CORBIS/Julie Houck

The People

About 25 million people live in Peru. Some are descendants of the Spanish rulers. Many more are relatives of the Incas or other Indian groups that lived long ago. Other Peruvians are **mestizos**. They have both Spanish and Indian backgrounds.

Family life is very important in Peru. In fact, many relatives from one family often live in the same house. Peruvians are friendly people who are very proud of their country and their backgrounds. Many have held onto their old ways of doing things, while others mix old and newer ways.

CORBIS/Galen Rowell

Hill Farmers Near Huallanca

A Guard At The Presidential Palace In Lima

CORBIS/The Purcell Team

Cuzco, The Former Capital Of The Inca Empire

CORBIS/Roman Sourmar

City life in Peru is much like city life in the United States. Cars zoom along busy streets while people walk on sidewalks. There are tall buildings, hotels, banks, and museums. There are many outdoor shops, too. Some Peruvian families live in apartments or homes. Poorer families often live in tiny houses made of cardboard or tin.

Away from the big cities, life in Peru is very different. Peruvians who live high in the Andes live much as their relatives did long ago. Many are farmers who live in small houses made of mud or stones. They even wear the same type of clothing their ancestors did.

Only a few groups of Indians live in the Amazon. These people live in small villages deep in the jungle. They hunt animals and live in huts just as they have for thousands of years.

CORBIS/Galen Rowell

The Busy Town Of Huaraz

Amazon
River

Huaraz

Cuzco

A House
On The
Upper
Amazon
River

Schoolgirls
In Uniform
In Piura

• Iquitos
• Piura

• Arequipa

Schools And Language

A Sign At A Medicinal Plant Shop At A Market In Iquitos

Children in Peru must go to school between the ages of 6 and 12. They learn basic subjects such as reading and math. Many country children are not able to go to school. Sometimes there aren't enough teachers. Other times, there aren't any schools nearby.

Many languages are spoken in Peru. Most Peruvians speak Spanish, especially in the large cities. Quechua is the ancient language of the Incas. It is spoken mainly by the Indians who live in the Andes. Some Quechua words are also used in the English language. "Llama," "puma," and "condor" are all Quechua words.

Many other languages are spoken in the Amazon. The small groups that live there often have their own special languages that are very old.

A Boy Studies At Home In Arequipa

CORBIS/Phil Schermeister

A Worker Holding Colorful Yarn At A Market In Lima

CORBIS/The Purcell Team

Many Peruvians are farmers. They grow crops such as sugarcane, coffee, and cotton. In the higher Andes areas, some people raise llamas or other animals. City Peruvians have different jobs. They work in offices, restaurants, shops, and markets.

Fishermen With Their Catch In Pacasmayo

CORBIS/Staffan Wildstrand

Tourism provides many jobs in Peru. In this job, Peruvians entertain visitors in their country. Every year, thousands of people visit Peru to see the beautiful Andes. They come to learn about the great Incas and see the buildings they built long ago. Some also come to visit the green Amazon rain forest.

CORBIS/Ric Ergenbright

Pacasmayo

★Lima

Chinchero

A Farmer Plowing A Field With Oxen In Chinchero

A Couple
Eating At A
Folklore Fiesta
Near Cuzco

Amazon
River

★Lima

•Cuzco

CORBIS/Caroline Penn

Peppers, Lemons, Tomatoes, And Carrots At A Lima Market

CORBIS/Dave Bartruff

Many Peruvian dishes are made with grains, peppers, and most of all, potatoes. Potatoes are used in everything from soups to main courses. Fruits are also popular in Peru. Pineapples, watermelons, oranges, and grapes are just some of the fruits people like to eat.

Fish On A Barbecue Near The Amazon River

Peruvians enjoy different meats, too. Pork, beef, and chicken dishes are all popular. Seafood is also a favorite, especially along the coast. One favorite dish is *ceviche* (seh-VEE-chay). It is fresh fish soaked in lemon or lime juice.

CORBIS/Wolfgang Kaehler

The Reenactment Of The Escape Of The Inca King During A Puno Carnival

CORBIS/Daniel Lane

The people of Peru love to dance and listen to music. They also love soccer, which is played in giant stadiums or country streets. Many people also like horse racing.

Basketball, volleyball, and baseball are favorite sports, too. Another special pastime is **bullfighting**. In this sport, a man stands in an area with a large bull. He waves a bright cape to make the bull angry. As the bull charges, the man moves out of the way. It takes a lot of bravery and skill to be a good bullfighter.

Christmas, Easter, and New Year's Day are three holidays that are celebrated in both Peru and the United States. Peruvians also have special holidays of their own. *Corpus Christi* is a religious holiday that many people celebrate in the city of Cuzco. Statues of saints are carried throughout the city as people sing and pray. Another special holiday is **Inti Raymi**. This huge festival is a very old Incan celebration. It is held at the beginning of winter to honor the Incan god of the sun.

Peru is a land of many differences. It is a place with wet jungles and dry deserts. It is also a place with tall mountains and deep canyons. There are old Incan ruins and new cities with noisy streets. If you like opposites, take a trip to Peru. You're sure to see many beautiful and wonderful things!

Street Musicians In Cuzco

CORBIS/Wolfgang Kaehler

CORBIS/Jonathan Blair

Lima
★
Huilloc● ●Cuzco
Puno ● ● Lake Titicaca

Area
About 500,000 square miles (1.3 million square kilometers)—a little smaller than Alaska.

Population
About 25 million people.

Capital City
Lima.

Other Important Cities
Arequipa, Callao, Iquitos, and Cuzco.

Money
The nuevo sol.

National Languages
Spanish and Quechua. Aymará is also spoken is some areas.

National Holiday
Independence Day on July 28.

National Song
"Himno Nacional," or "National Anthem."

National Flag
Two red stripes with a white stripe between them. Peru's coat of arms is in the middle of the white stripe. The coat of arms has pictures of a llama, a tree, and a yellow horn with gold coins spilling out of it.

Head of Government
The president of Peru.

Naymlap, A Half-Man, Half-Bird God, On A Ceremonial Spoon In A Lima Museum

Peru Trivia

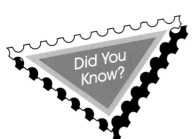

Did You Know?

Peru is really called "The Republic of Peru." People just say "Peru" for short.

Lake Titicaca in southern Peru is the highest navigable lake in the world. "Navigable" means that the lake is deep and wide enough for ships to sail on it. Lake Titicaca sits 12,530 feet above the level of the ocean.

The white potato that many people eat today was first grown in the Andes. The Incas learned how to grow them as crops, cook them, and store them. Today, many different types of potatoes can be found in Peru. They come in all sorts of colors—even blue, purple, yellow, and brown!

In the Andes near Cuzco, the ruins of **Machu Picchu** (MAH–choo PEEK–choo) sit high on a mountaintop. This ancient village was built by the Incas long ago. Since the village was built at the top of a mountain, the Spanish invaders never found it. Even after all these years, many of the buildings and stairways of Machu Picchu are still standing.

How Do You Say?

	SPANISH	HOW TO SAY IT
Hello	hola	(OH–lah)
Good-bye	adiós	(ah–dee–OHS)
Please	por favor	(POR fah–VOR)
Thank You	gracias	(GRAH–see–uss)
One	uno	(OO–noh)
Two	dos	(DOHS)
Three	tres	(TRACE)
Peru	Perú	(peh–ROO)

alpacas (al–PA–kuhz)
An alpaca is an animal that lives in the Andes mountains of Peru. Alpacas are related to camels and have warm, woolly fur.

bullfighting (BULL–fye–ting)
Bullfighting is a popular sport in Peru. In this pastime, a man stands in an area with a bull and waves a cape at it. When the bull charges, the man quickly moves out of the way.

civilizations (sih–vih–lih–ZAY–shunz)
Civilizations are large societies with cities, governments, and written languages. The earliest civilization in Peru was created by the Chavín Indians.

continent (KON–tih–nent)
Most of the land areas on Earth are divided up into huge sections called continents. Peru is located on the continent of South America.

Inca (ING–kah)
The Inca Indians created one of the most important civilizations in Peru. The Incas were great warriors and ruled a large part of South America at one time.

Inti Raymi (IN–tee RAY–mee)
Inti Raymi is an Incan festival celebrated every year in the city of Cuzco. It is an ancient celebration to honor the Incan god of the sun.

Machu Picchu (MAH–choo PEEK–choo)
Machu Picchu is an ancient village built long ago by the Incas. Since it sits on the top of a mountain, the village wasn't found for hundreds of years.

mestizos (meh–STEE–zohs)
Mestizos are people who have relatives from different backgrounds. Some Peruvians are mestizos with Spanish and Indian backgrounds.

rain forest (RAYN FOR–est)
A rain forest is a thick jungle where it rains often. Much of Peru is covered by the Amazon rain forest.

tourism (TOOR–ih–zem)
Tourism is the business of bringing travelers to a country and showing them around. Tourism is an important business in Peru.

Index

Web Sites

Learn more about Peru:
http://www.interknowledge.com/peru/index.html
http://www.peru-explorer.com

Learn more about Machu Picchu:
http://www.gorp.com/gorp/location/latamer/peru/machu.htm

Follow a search for frozen Inca mummies:
http://www.pbs.org/wgbh/nova/peru

Learn how to say some colors and numbers in Quechua:
http://www.andes.org/count.html

Listen to Peru's national anthem:
http://www.emulateme.com/sounds/peru.mid